NOT QUITE TASMANIAN

DEMELZA

Contents

Not Quite Bush Tucker
    Tim Tam Temptation   9
    Queen of the Leftovers   11
    Wallaby with Henk and George   12
    Tea   16
    A Nice Hot Cup of Tea   17
    I Wonder if it's Chlorinated?   19
    C Omissions Diet   22
    Eggs Benedict   23

Almost Country
    Be Careful in your Conversation   27
    Dolphin Sands   29
    To Kingston One Way   31
    Wish You Were Here   33
    Princess Park   35
    The South Hobart Tip Shop – I Love You   37
    The Shack   39
    Mel's Jog   42
    Hooray for Hobart's New Improved Car Park!?!   44
    A New Beginning   46
    Beauty in the Blaze   47

Fashion and Passion

Ode to the Tasmanian Puffer Jacket	51
Bogue	52
Did you just call me fat?	54
Mirror	55
Praise for Penny (and her Poise)	56

Are We There Yet?

Free To Good Home – Flu – Only One Owner	61
No Play Today	63
Nano Nap	66
Multitasking	67
Snippet	69

Death and Despair

Dear Mary,	75
Reflections	76
Do You Hear Me Calling	78
As You Take Your Final Breath	80
Laundry Day	82
Decisions	84
My Little Girl	86
Flesh Wound	90
Can You Tell Me?	92
Hold Your Breath 100	96

Retirement	101
Poppy was a Soldier	103
'Hey Mel'	104
This Generation	105
Mere Hobbyist	106

My People, Birth and Celebrations

What I really want for Christmas	111
Avocado Kisses	113
Birth	115
Sitting Here Waiting	116
I've Been Christmas Shopping	117
See this?	119
Best Intentions	120

Not Quite Educated

Memoirs of the undiagnosed Dyslexic	125
I want to be a poet	127
Predicate Etiquette	129
I Often Got My Letters Wrong	130
Precipitation	132
The Bookcase – A Collective Noun in a Thousand Words	
	133
Run On	139
Procrastination	141
Just a Mum	143

Not Quite Bush Tucker

Tim Tam Temptation

I knew they were on special
But I was well prepared
I'd skip the bickie aisle
And buy some fruit instead

But they stacked 'em by the entrance
With the veg – in aisle one!
And they jumped into my trolley
The battle had begun!

It was well past breakfast time
But nearing morning tea
I found myself in aisle four
Devouring number three

I threw in cans of mushrooms
I tossed in sauce and pasta
My self-control had left the store
My mission cried disaster

The fourth one took me by surprise
When I was looking for the bread
The baker gave a knowing smile
My face grew rather red

So now I felt embarrassment
Guilt and mortal shame
The Tim Tams had the upper hand
They were masters at this game

I opened up the freezer door
And nearly shoved them in
I felt the floor staff stalking me
Was there chockie on my chin?

I carried on down aisle nine
Candles brooms and acetone
Nappy pins and medicines
'Twas then I heard my phone

And in that moment of distraction
I picked up one or two
Now five and six had crossed my lips
And I'd hardly had to chew

As I hurried to the checkout
My plight had left me three
Would they make it to the car park?
Tune in next week and see

Queen of the Leftovers

Toast to crumbs
Crumbs to fish
Fish to pie
Pie to dish
Dish to fry
With sauce of course
Nothing left to feed the horse

Roast to bake
Bake to mash
Mash to pie
Pie to dish
Dish to fry
With sauce again
Nothing left to feed the hen

Scraps to pot
Pot to soup
Soup to sauce
Sauce to gloop
Gloop to gravy
Feed the gravy to the baby
Nothing left to feed the navy

Wallaby with Henk and George
In memory of Henk Meerding and George O'Brien – the
first of the fossickers

When Nan first told this story
I laughed and thought a while
Not sure if I believed her
But it rather made me smile

They used to go out camping
That's George and Henk his mate
They'd start down here in Geeveston
Leave through the garden gate

They never took a vehicle
Well you couldn't way back then
And tracks were laid for 'sissies'
Both George and Henk were men

The ways they went were deep and thick
No path for cart or horse
Their rucksacks filled with sustenance
And rifle shot of course

Henk and George enjoyed the bush
Loved fossicking about
Both were keen on natural things
Of that there was no doubt

George a fine photographer
Compiled photos to impress
Images of plants and fauna
Our history more or less

Sometimes they'd 'hit the bush'
For days or even weeks
They'd take their gear and disappear
Seeking gemstones in the creeks

You could call them naturalists
Explorers – legendarians
But one thing you could never say
Was the boys were vegetarians

The first week they were 'out'
They'd eat the food they'd brought
Then they'd shoot a bit of this or that
And enjoy the game they caught

Wallaby was easy fare
There were such a lot about
And wallaby was good to eat
Of that they had no doubt

Their diet was established
Entree, mains, dessert
What was left they ate for supper
At night the bones were burnt

Wallaby for breakfast,
Lunch and morning tea
Every time the billy boiled
They'd dine on wallaby

But after they had eaten it
For three weeks in a row
Henk felt the urge for something else
Something sweet you know

So when they left the bush
Past the road down near the mill
They headed for the nearest shop
The Store in Huonville

Henk was up for something fresh
With flavour, crunch and smell
He was done with stale crackers
And wallaby as well

He nearly jumped a fence
When he saw a cherry tree
But thought the better of it
Henk's a gentleman you see

At the store he was delighted
With the peaches well displayed
Pulled some coins from out his pocket
And soon the bill was paid

Then Henk turned to George and asked
'What will your order be?'
'Three patties, mate,' said George to Henk
'And make them wallaby!'

Tea

The peasants drink simplicit-tea
The King and Queen their royal-tea
God of course drinks sovereign-tea
His subjects down their loyal-tea

The gov'ment swill ambiguit-tea
The foolish slurp stupidit-tea
The merciless serve brutalit-tea
Whereas the dreamer gags realit-tea

Heroes toast their vanit-tea
The oldies their infirmit-tea
The righteous lap-up puri-tea
While philosophers share humanit-tea

I water down insanit-tea
And fail to serve humilit-tea
But the tea I seek most fervently
Is the elusive cup of tranquilit-tea

A Nice Hot Cup of Tea

The day it started early
The car was low on fuel
I had to pack their lunches
We were nearly late for school

So I'm looking forward to sitting
With a nice hot cup of tea
Perhaps I'll put my feet up
And have some time for me

But while the kettle's boiling
I'll hang the washing out
And pick up all the pegs
That someone's spread about

Then I'll sit down with my cuppa
'Cause I like it good and hot
And if there's nothing to distract me
It'll really hit the spot

But first I'll do the dishes
'Cause then I can relax
The kids have walked some mud in
So I'll quickly mop their tracks

Now while my tea is brewing
I'll run out to the mail
And quickly grab the washing in
Before it starts to hail

Oh, someone left the gate open
And the dog's gone up the path
I wonder what he's rolling in?
He'll have to have a bath!

And I'll pop this load of washing on
The dog was pretty smelly
And I'll have to clean the washtub out
Before it turns to jelly

So now I stand here gulping
A tepid cup of tea
I have to down it pretty quick
'Cause the kids leave school at three!

I Wonder if it's Chlorinated?

The RSVPs have all returned
I have them in my hand
I'll fax them to the restaurant
The food it shall be grand

Of course there is the problem
With the Frazer's middle boy
Seems he has an allergy
To anything with soy

And Uncle Ben can't tolerate
Anything with dairy
Affects his small intestinals
The outcome's rather scary

Young Richie won't eat meat
Be it red or white or fish
I'm very sure they'll offer him
Some other kind of dish

I'll check the list for vegans
Looks like quite a table
Nigel, Nell and Aunty Shell
And Shirley's Cousin Mabel

Now Jazzy can't have gluten
(She's a coeliac)
And we'll want to cut out carbies
To keep sweet with Aunty Jacque

Simon can't eat cashew nuts
And Micky can't eat wheat
It stuffs up his intolerance
Or was that Uncle Pete?

No cumin for our Matthew
His reaction is severe
They say it's anaphylactic
A condition not so rare

No bananas, tomatoes or apricots
For Nana Tilly Palace
That's way too much potassium
(You know she's on dialysis)

And remember Uncle Thomas?
The one who's got the goat
It's the onions and the apples
That gives him all the bloat

No mushrooms for our brother Tim
He's as sickly as a biscuit
I've seen the mess that he can make
I'm just not prepared to risk it

Aunt Ruby Jane (the fussy one)
Can't stomach any greens
Be they rocket, chives, asparagus
Or any kind of beans

The restaurant just got back to me
They've done everything they oughta
But all they have to offer us
Is carrot sticks and water!

C Omissions Diet

Cheese, chocolate, chicken and chips
I swear this day shall not pass my lips

Everything else starting with 'C'
I now declare is bad for me!

Cakes and cookies, crackles and creams
From this time forth are fading dreams

Candies and crepes make no mistake
Are now deleted from my intake

Cheesecakes, chops and coconut rough
Shall not be remembered when times are tough

I've taken a vow to eat nothing with 'C'
Unless of course it's good for me

Like carrots and cabbage and little cumquats
Celery, cucumber and chillies (not hot)

Except for the veggies without calories
I'll stick to my diet "Omission of C's"

Eggs Benedict
Dedicated to every mother who has ever had to sit and wait

She dissects her egg with the skill of a surgeon
Proficiently peeling back layers of white to expose a fragile
transparent skin covering the fluid yolk
Willing her knife to move slowly
Deliberately
Daring not to puncture the membrane pathetically
protecting the golden liquid

Poised on a fork the yolk reaches her mouth, contents
spilling
Running indiscriminately over her taste buds
Void of control
Subject now to the reflex action of the swallowing muscle

All too soon the taste disappears

Hollandaise sauce efficiently mopped up and devoured with
sourdough bread
The last flavour left will be the salty taste of cold bacon

The fast broken
Mother waits
As the neurosurgeon performs a spinal operation on her child

Almost Country

Be Careful in your Conversation

Is it just imagination?
Or my objective observation
That anywhere around this nation
I will find a lost relation
Or work colleague who's on vacation
Or her best friend from his flirtation?

If I attend a graduation
Or any other celebration
That requires of me an invitation
Then there will be an expectation
That I will know the congregation

But please hear my tribulation
Indulge with me this fierce frustration
My increasing need for liberation
Pertaining to our new foundation

When I have a reservation
With my man for mastication
Please give us some consideration
We do not need investigation

Inherently our population
Is not in fear of isolation
I have to say this revelation
Has given me a hesitation

And guided me in conversation
It seems we have a generation
That's organised by speculation
And – two degrees of separation!

Dolphin Sands

Ok Mister Wordsworth
Forget the daffodils
There's an awful lot of pleasure
In Swansea's sandy hills

When I lie upon my couch
In tired or pensive mood
My inward eye is taken by
A coastline barely viewed

Eagles soar in skies above
Seagulls swoop below
Pipers hide in marram grass
Where boobialla grow

Edward Lear tear out your hair
Discard your runcible spoon
Settle here on the edge of the sand
And dance by the light of the moon

Your pig would wallow without squalor
He wouldn't need a shilling
I am sure he'd find the warm lagoon
Luscious and fulfilling

Had Banjo ever crossed the Strait
He'd have followed sound advice
I'm sure he'd fall in love with all
From Swansea's paradise

All I can say of Dolphin Sands
Is when can I return?
My heart is captured by this place
For it my soul doth yearn

To Kingston One Way

The day was warm and wonderful
And I was traveling light
A kayak and a paddle
Would float me there alright

I knew, 'the farther off from England
The nearer is to France'
But did it not seem way too far
When the waves began to dance?

And the sun flickered on the water
And the wet suit grew too tight
And I had to keep on paddling
Keep perspective in my sight

When all at once I vomited
And fed the fish full score
Then paddling turned to challenging
Each stroke became a chore

But paddle on I did
To achieve my destination
I'd like to say to joyful crowds
Sending up a grand ovation

But there was no one there to greet me
And probably just as well
I didn't look my 'very best'
And gave off a fishy smell

I hauled the kayak up the beach
Left it high above the foam
And wobbled to the roadside
Where I caught the bus back home

Wish You Were Here

Wish you were here
The tent's got a rip
The mossies are hungry
We jammed the new zip

Wish you were here
The kids are all sick
One missed the bucket
The other was quick

Wish you were here
It's rained every day
The bedding's all wet
The children can't play

Wish you were here
I dropped the phone in the water
The child was falling
'Twas lucky I caught her

Wish we were home
Where the bath's good and hot
Here's plenty of water
But hot it is not

Wish you were here
You could play in the mess
There's mud on our clothes
In our food – what a stress!

Wish you were here
You missed all the fun
No one got burnt
Least not by the sun

Wish you were here
The kids are both better
Apart from the rash
I described in the letter

Wish we were with you
Out of the rain
Camping without you
Never again

Princess Park

I am the Pirate Princess
See me sailing through the park
My flags are flying high and free
Children scramble to embark

The children are the pirates
They sail the seven seas
Eat chips from paper bags
Plunder cakes and mouldy cheese

Shoeless sprites with boundless life
Discarding cares and all
Forlornly hauled from endless play
If mums or dads should call

The nameless crew performs as one
As they conquer hidden foes
Scuffing up my sandy floors
With bare and grubby toes

My mast is high, my sails are set
The leaves blow round in a gust
The hammock swings as high as it can
Stirring the midsummer dust

Kids walk the plank
And run the ring
And from off my slide
I see somebody swing

And I know for sure
They've had a great day
Repeatedly saying
'Best park in the Bay!'

The South Hobart Tip Shop – I Love You

There's nothing you can't find
If you really put your mind
To look beyond the borders of the norm
You could make yourself a cactus
Using cardboard poles for practise
And have yourself a decent desert storm

For three or four bucks each
One year we saved a peach
An' bought ourselves some classy Christmas trees
Our super fun display
Had next to no decay
Was somewhat green and free from allergies

Once we bought a tent
I'll admit the poles were bent
But the zipper was in perfect working order
We camped out in the hills
Safe from winter chills
And in summertime we lent it to our daughter

Today I bought a power pack
Completely tested out the back
It was just the thing that I was looking for
I gave the right amount of money
Felt as warm as toast and honey
And now I'm charging up just like I did before!

If you really have a nose
You may find a garden hose
Or things to make yourself a chicken coop
There'll be knives and forks and butter
Somewhere beneath the clutter
You may even find a pot for making soup

Now if you have a doubt
As to what it's all about
Take a look up there yourself and see
You could find yourself a cycle
Be impressed by their recycle
And I'm sure you'll love that place as much as me

The Shack

The noise it woke us from our dreams
It thundered through our heads
What could rock the room so much
And torment us in our beds?

The sound was like a train a comin'
A booming down the track
Where was the nearest railway?
We were camped out in the shack!

Could it be a thunderstorm
A brewing up a treat?
I bunkered down, blocked my ears
But rest was short not sweet

The noise it penetrated
And rolled about the room
The others felt the shaking
And someone grabbed the broom

They poked the roaring snorer
And yelled at him to quit
There was silence for a moment
And we settled down a bit

By morning we were edgy
Our smiles drawn on tight
Bloodshot, blurry eyeballs
By gum we looked a sight!

We sat there sipping coffee
Lamenting up a din
When all at once the door's ajar
The snorer walks on in

You lot all look glum he says
As he pulls up next to us
This camping is a breeze he says
Don't know why you make a fuss

All those words incite us
To get our honour back
That night when he's a snoring
We drag him from the shack

We set his lilo out to float
On the local water hole
We push it to the middle
Use a gum tree as a pole

Sniggers form around our lips
As we climb back to our beds
Visions of him getting wet
Are floating through our heads

The sun shone in our cabin
With a start we all awoke
To find out what had happened
To our thoughtless little joke

We cried out with a passion
As our van roared out of view
The sod had nicked our vehicle
There was nothing we could do!

There's no moral to this story
Just a weary walk to town
And a warning from the snorer
'TWAS LUCK I DIDN'T DROWN!'

Mel's Jog

Left right
Left right
Seven thirty
Dark night
Dead bird
On trail
Post box
Junk mail
Left right
Left right
Sharp bend
In sight
Mind gutter
Rain in face
Keeping up a
Good pace
Smell hedge
Feel breeze
Itchy nose
Don't sneeze
Bus stop
Thirty three
Slight pain
Left knee

Up hill
Round bend
Two k's
Till end
Smell roast
Smell beer
Past pub
Smokers near
Destination
In sight
Down hill
Feeling light
Five k's
That's it for me
Slowing down
It's eight o' three

Hooray for Hobart's New Improved Car Park!?!

A bit exciting really
Lots more parking spaces
Equals happy people
With smiles upon their faces

They're open now till ten
A more convenient hour
Means access to the hospital
And to the people power

There's just one small point to note
It fair confuses me
The ramps and levels don't match up
I lost my car you see

Well the builder pointed out
The floors they all have colours
Wow I hadn't noticed that
(Unlike all you others)

Next time I parked my car
I noted 'colour green'
I wouldn't lose my spot again
I'm brighter than I seem

Alas, alack I can't believe
There's egg upon my face
Three levels are a shade of green
This is a crazy place

Light green, dark green, medium
Woolworths you are to blame
For ever more I'll park my car
Outside – in the rain!

A New Beginning

We watch the fires glow
Disturbingly in the distance
Under a cloud
Illuminated by a rose-coloured lining

Morning brings a red sun
Shining like a perpetual full moon
On the horizon of a replayed movie
We pray for precipitation
And run out to the clothes line
As the rain begins to fall

But is it over there?
Past the safety of the Derwent

Our clothes smell
Like a New Year's Eve party at Murdunna
And soft flakes of ash fall gently into our iced teas
As we update our status
We wonder if the old shack still stands
In Sommers Bay

Our hearts' anguish

It's been a long week for some
And a new beginning isn't even in sight

Beauty in the Blaze

Light beams of orange
Falling on terracotta tiles
Mesmerising all who stop to gaze

The sun playing she is the moon
Her pretentious beauty too bright to fool us

Large flakes of ash wisped gently about by unseen breaths
Morphing into smudges by the most gentle of fingers

Fields of enchanted grain growing as golden as a fairy tale
And as deceptive as the witch of west

Mountains become pale blue silhouettes
Disappearing as the smoke haze thickens

All the dangers hidden by the hills
Creating an illusion of beauty in the blaze

Fashion and Passion

Ode to the Tasmanian Puffer Jacket

Tassie had a problem, the weather was the reason
They solved it with 'The Puffer', a skin for any season

Gen Y, Gen X or pensioner, there's no discrimination
They'll wear it to a footy match or year 12 graduation

They dress it up, they dress it down, and no one looks a dag
And when, of course, they're not in use, they squash it in a bag!

I've seen them in their slippers and those fluffy, wuffy boots
I've seen them in their high heels, and no one gives a hoot

Sunnies and a 'Puffer', shorts and sandals too
They wear it on the beaches, and at the bar-b-que
Feather filled or Dacron, it looks as comfy as can be
If I ever move to Tassie, I'll buy one just to see!

Bogue

I wanna be a Bogan
Enough of wearing shoes
I'm sick of fancy fashion
With all its have-to-do's

I wanna pair of ugg boots
(Or cheapish look-a-likes)
I wanna wear me trackies
Ditch the Pradas and the Nikes
They always look so happy
Like they've just rolled out of bed
Yes I'd like to be as comfy
But I'm stuck in shoes instead

I'm practising my protocol
'Looking better than the rest'
Often quite uncomfortable
Forever 'dressed for best'

If I could be a Bogan
Just for a-half-a day
I'm sure you can appreciate
The passion I display

Fashion is a fickle thing
That makes me wanna cry!
Can't I kick my heels off
Just once before I die?

Don't think of me a snob
From the social upper class
I'm trying to reform
Stick my birthright in my past

I'm not a troublemaker
Nor the least bit of a rogue
Please heed my fashion mantra
Let's make Bogan Vogue!

Did you just call me fat?

Call me larger than the average
Stout or things like that
Comfortable or spreading
Anything but fat!

The 'f' word's far too harsh to use
So label me well-rounded
Chunky, stacked or strapping
My bones are strongly grounded

I like to think I'm cuddly
Generous or plump
But never call me fatty
Or even heffalump!

There's more of me to love
There's extra to go around
Plentiful and scrumptious
Have such a luscious sound

A rose by any other name
Will still smell as sweet as me
I may be well proportioned
But fat I'll never be!

Mirror

Magic mirror on the wall
You make me look so thin and tall
Yet when I leave this fitting room
I know my size will fairly bloom

Although I think myself as thin
It's only 'cause I'm sucking in
And when a window catches me
I am surprised at what I see

So let me see myself for real
No matter what I think or feel
It is surely true and wise
To love myself at any size

Praise for Penny (and her Poise)
Dedicated to ... well I can't say can I!

I read the ad on the side of a bus
About women one in three
Who are subject to experiences
That would disable you or me

The reasons they may vary
But the outcome seems the same
A puddle on the floor
And a face hung down in shame

But Penny's got the answer
(Names here have been changed)
(Places, dates and photographs)
(Have all been rearranged)

Now Penny's got the answer
She always comes prepared
In case she has a coughing fit
Or chokes on garlic bread

She doesn't cross her legs
Or race out to the loo
Cause Penny's wearing Poise tonight
And that she says will do!

Other brands are common
But Penny says inferior
"You've got to get the Poise dears
They really are superior"

So if you're scared to sneeze
And you're the one in three
Think of Penny and her Poise dear
Go buy a pack and see!

Are We There Yet?

Free To Good Home – Flu – Only One Owner

I've had this jolly flu now
So long I can't remember
If I picked it up in May
Or early last November?

It's followed me around and
I'm out of ways to shake it
I even saw a doctor
Who said she would not take it

I've fed it lemon juice and grape fruit
And lots of chicken soup
But this flu is just too comfortable
It will not leave the coop

I've been gargling salt and garlic
Dosed up on vitamin C
I've even phoned the people
Who said they'd pray for me

But this here jolly flu
Just will not leave the nest
So I'll take it back to bed again
And try to get some rest

Now if you know someone
Who likes to stay at home
And loves a bit of sickness
Could you ring them on your phone

Tell them it's for sale
And it's going really cheap
It loves a low immunity
And thrives on lack of sleep

I'll be happy for the caller
To remove it from my place
Or I'll arrange delivery
With Bell's or Brothers Grace

If the buyers want to call in
And sit about for tea
I promise that I'll sneeze on them
And offload this flu for free

No Play Today

We'd done the beach
We'd done the hills
We'd tipped our drinks
And left the spills

We'd fetched the water
In a leaky tin
Tossed apple cores
And missed the bin

Stashed our shoes
And half our socks
Dropped wet towels
And collected rocks

The Mumma said
"This is enough"
Clean out this car
Collect your stuff

This vehicle smells
Like a public zoo
The neighbour's cat
And doggy doo

Unless it's clean
This very day
None of you
Shall think of play

With vinegar rags
And soda supplied
Siobhan laughed
While Maxine cried

We discovered where
The sun screen went
Max had squeezed it
Through a vent

Found felt-tip pens
A library book
Ten feathers from
The neighbour's chook

Found food enough
To feed nine mice
Yoghurt smudges
That tasted nice

Weet-Bix cards
A notebook too
Unfortunately
All wet through

Took us longer
Than an hour
Afterwards
We had to shower

Unjam the vaccy
Wash our pants
Hose away
Unwanted ants

So now the car
Is shiny bright
The mumma's happy
And we're alright

Nano Nap

Foot prints on the toilet seat
Toothpaste on the floor
Tissues in the fish bowl
Sunscreen on the door

Fingerprints were everywhere
Max's working no doubt
She'd cleaned the loo with denture paste
And then not hung about

Toilet paper trailed from
The front door to the back
'Twas wound around each block of wood
Then laid neatly in a stack

I found her at the clothes line
Rigging up a swing
With Nanna's favourite sweater
And a broken teething ring

I had to give her credit
She'd kept herself amused
While I'd sat down exhausted
And had accidently snoozed!

Multitasking

Doing one thing at a time
It is not!
Taxing on the brain?
Yes a lot
We wake up every morning
With such a lot to do
Prepare the bread
Make the bed
Put the baby on the loo
Kids here
Kids there
Washing hanging everywhere
Fold it up
Stack it high
Hang it out and let it dry
Meantime read the storybooks
Sweep the floors and
Feed the chooks
Check the mail and
(While still on line)
Flick through the site that's selling wine
Burp the baby
Change his pants
Find the Wiggles
Let's have a dance

And while we do
We'll pick up toys
Cook some muffins
Enjoy the noise
Watch the babe with the back of our head
Stir white sauce
And slice the bread
Think about tomorrow's meals
Check how hot the bath tub feels
Listen to them learn their tables
Check their spelling
Make some labels
Feed the baby on my knee
Wow
Let's all stop for morning tea

Snippet

'I am going to smoke and drink until I don't even care anymore'

They laugh as they pass the doorway of the Save the Children's Shop

They may not care but I wish they'd consider the people who do

My mind is on Mother – her walls dripping in nicotine orange

Ribs as brittle as her decrepit net curtains, barely able to move, stress fractures forming every time she coughs

Constantly in pain

Constantly short of breath

Unable to clean – too proud for help

But we give her no choice and have her removed from the premises while we scrape mould and grime off walls and benches

We superficially conquer the kitchen and bathroom
But please don't open a cupboard

Mum returns and is mortified at the sight of the missing net curtains

Mum they were ripped they would not have survived a wash and I'm going to Spotlight tomorrow to replace them

No you are not

Yes I am

Where are they

In the rubbish

Where's the rubbish bag

I burnt it, I lie, I'm as stubborn as Mother

Later I find money tucked into my wallet

Dad cooks despite his cancer

He is grateful for our cleaning

Maybe he will invite friends inside for a cuppa

I live a plane trip away and my three day weekend is spent saturating myself in a nicotine haze

I let the kids spend our last day in their pyjamas and slip them into uncontaminated clothing as we enter the car for the airport

I buy toys and clothes for the kids from Save the Children's shop with her money

I regret that I cannot interject into the conversation that so quickly passes the door.

*

Death and Despair

Dear Mary,

I see you sitting in your chair
Surrounded with your many books
The wagtails outside flit from grass to tree
You cannot see the mountain from where you sit
But you know it's there
Watching

I miss you Mary

You taught me poems
Corrected my spelling and
Inspired me to learn

You shared your family with me and
Asked after mine

I loved you because you cared
You encouraged me
Your laughter was always friendly

You are no longer here
Now Mary

But I still love you

Reflections

Can't stop myself from thinking
The words keep tumbling through
Can't live my life without the thoughts
The thoughts of losing you

I am inept
I have regret
Can't accept you dying
If I reflect this hard concept
I lose respect – start crying

If I should stop the driven rain
From falling through the skies
Then I should hold the key to stop
The floodgates of my eyes

The warm sun keeps on shining
Dew dissipates to mist
Green sprouts will haze this earth again
Where creation's mouth has kissed

Your desire flows into my soul
Your legacy is mine
Let truth foresee my destiny
As love and hope combine

Although inept
I'll not regret
The process of you dying
When I reflect your last request
I look up and keep on trying

Do You Hear Me Calling

Don't seem to have the courage
To remove your number from my phone
I press the buttons vaguely
Listening for the tone

Do you hear me calling?
Do you hear me calling?

You don't answer
You don't answer
You don't answer me

Do you even know I'm missing you?

Memories cannot fill
The void within my heart
I know I have to carry on
Just don't know how to start
Picked up the phone today
Says your number's not in use
I cried again and tried again
Will I always be confused?

Do you hear me calling?
Do you hear me calling?

You don't answer
You don't answer
You don't answer me
Do you even know I'm missing you?

As You Take Your Final Breath

I want to be so mad at you
For all the pain you put me through
But when I see you lying there
My thoughts of anger disappear
I sit with you this last night
Your body bent
Your hands clenched tight
Your eyes flit from clock to moon
The witching hour comes too soon
In agitation you sit and rock
Eyes on moon, eyes on clock
The hour comes and then it goes
Your body stressed
Your soul exposed
Delusion weaves a stingy knot
You stare at things that I cannot
What gives you hope or satisfaction?
What could ease your vain distraction?
Squint your eyes, adjust your glasses
Time ticks on, night-time passes
You are confused, you're agitated
Stolen moments, death's abated

But it comes – it still comes

And as the cock begins to crow
Your breaths become more rare – more slow
Finally you breathe your last
What was now – is now the past
And I cry....
        and I cry....
               and I cry

Laundry Day

Disjointed
Inconsistent
Life drifting anxiously about me
Hopelessness catching me unawares
Like articles of washing hanging on a line
Some days floating merrily with the breeze
Other days just hanging in there
At times being whipped around and around by driving winds
Being carried along by the whims of others
Never making a choice of my own
Others always knowing what's best for me
Tea towels wrapped too tightly against the wire
Fraying on exposed ends
Ripping as I pull them from their captor
Decisions tearing me apart
Life seems extreme
Clothes gather together in smelly piles
Lights, darks, fluffies, permanent press
Moulded into human-less forms
Waiting despondently for their turn
Full or half cycle
Fast or slow spin
No enjoyment
No sense of achievement

Just another thing to be done
Another have to do
A necessary domestication to be ticked off a malodourous perpetual list
Today the sun permeates my skin
The sensual pleasure lifts my soul
Plastic pegs play tin soldiers
Steadfast at their posts
But expendable if dropped or broken
Pieces of colour protruding from the mud
Visible but not significant
Not enough to dirty my imperfect finger nails
The day completes
Fresh towers of soft folds competing for space in the basket
Medicated, balanced, safe
Socks against undies
Towels against socks
Pressure, but no pain
Always within a boundary
I wonder what would happen if I didn't launder for one day?
If the nappies and dishcloths were silent
If the clothes stayed clean and undemanding
Would I miss it?
My basket overflows

Decisions

We were simply out of toilet paper
Nothing more than that
No extravagance
Small amount of waste perhaps
Could have thought we were surviving the side effects of a curry overdose
Sneezing fits or infectious bladder
But we weren't
We were simply out of toilet paper
What is the average?
The expected quota?
Our lot – three rolls per day
(Not including the ones down stairs beneath our house who shop upstairs when desperate – if you know what I mean.)
So here I stand in front of the shop display, trolley empty, void of children
And the simple act of buying toilet paper becomes a situation of complexity beyond my capacity to understand
Excuse me could you move your trolley please?
Oh I'm sorry – can you go around?
Are you ok?
I'm fine!
Excuse me you are blocking the aisle – would you mind moving?
2 ply – 3ply – 4 bloody ply – single ply – recycled – from what?

No go around!
Extra strength – waffle weave – do we get fries with that?
Scented – quilted – floral – seasonally printed – sounds like butt wiping on Gran's pillow slip
Economy – unscented – unbleached – deconstructed – sarcasm added!
I just want some toilet paper
We are out of toilet paper!
Special – classic – double length – triple length – king-size
Aloe Vera – hypo allergenic – flushable – thank God for that!
Phone rings
What do you want?
Can we come for dinner…can we bring something?
Yes, yes
Toilet paper – we are out of toilet paper

My Little Girl

Surprised
As two red shoes and a matching plastic wallet slide into my view
Startled
As I look up to see a male police officer tackling a teenage girl to the ground
– not rough – just matter of fact
Cautious
As I step sideways to direct my child into our car
Thoughtful
As I observe the scene unfold before of me
Amazed
As a female officer accuses her of taking the drugs again
Curious
As the teenage girl insistently denies her accusation with words that hiss and seethe on the ground
Interested
To understand the relationship between the girl and the officer
Confronted
As I realise both driveways for my exit are blocked by police cars
– one conventionally parked
– the other facing oncoming traffic
Indifferent

As another officer offers an apology for my dilemma
Casual
As I respond – I can find another way
Concerned
As my young daughter, strapped, in the back seat declares
– I don't like that man
Cold
As I reply – he's just doing his job
Relieved
As the driveways clear and we follow the teenage girl and her entourage back onto the street
Angry
When I see you
And you
And you standing at the bus stop
Laughing
Is this fiasco entertaining?
Are you nervous for your friend?
Are you relieved it is her and not you?
Are you all high?
Why she is the only one in the car?
What power does she have to control the work day of five officers and two government vehicles?
Did she steal?
Yell obscenities?

Or is she your scape goat?
Today's distraction from your indifferent lives?
Confused
I drive
Anxiously
I pray – I pray that this time it would be different for the teenage girl
That there would be a change in her life
A new beginning
That she would know better friends than you
That she would know a mum and a dad who care
And that if this could not be true, that she would know someone else who does care
Like an Aunt or a Grandma
And if there is no Aunt or Grandma that somehow, someone who does care would find her
Someone who would believe in her and would know her full potential
Someone who would show her love
And that if you were ever to meet her – you would be the one
The one that would encourage her and inspire her
The one that would tell her she is worthy
The one she would believe

And I pray that these things might not take long to pass
And that I might have a change of heart towards her old
friends at the bus stop

Suddenly
I am overwhelmed
I pull over unable to drive through my tears
Stunned
I look to the back to see my five-year-old kick off her shoes
And shake the play money out of her
Red plastic wallet

Flesh Wound

Surface scratch
Hardly hurts at all

Stub toe
No blood
Just dull pain
Not deep

Graze
Brush off the gravel
Pick yourself up and carry on
Hardly any skin gone
Sunshine and fresh air

Paper cut hurts like hell
Sharp
But only temporary

Clean cut
Deep searing through seven layers
Mends fast – no infection
Forgotten sooner than a bruise

Peel back the skin
The corner of a tin shed
Broken bamboo
A nail rip

Deeper still
Where flesh cannot be replaced
Fast moving mechanical equipment
Grabbing to the bone
Permanent indentation
Obvious scar

Broken heart
Ripped in pieces
Strewn haphazardly on ground
Trampled underfoot
Forgotten about by all
But the bearer – who can never protect all the fragments

Can You Tell Me?
Spinal awareness week

Can you tell me what it's like
To step from an aeroplane and
Fall freely through the sky?
What do you feel
When you pull the cord and
The fabric blooms out behind you
Catching the tension in the air?

Can you tell me what it's like
To swim in the ocean with waves crashing all around
Foam spraying in your face?
Where mermaids snorkel in the waters
When the waves are calm?

Can you tell me what it's like
To stand on the edge of a cliff and
Piss?
Or to feel a girl's body
Pressed against your own?
I can't feel these things
Because my neck was broken

I can tell you what it's like
To see lights veering towards you in a car
I can tell you what it's like
To hear my sister screaming
Beside me in the back seat

I can tell you how it feels
To wake in a hospital bed
With no one to comfort you
But a father grieving for his wife

I can tell you of a sister
A scared and lonely girl
Who will never have her mother

I was eleven
You were twenty-one
I am twenty one today

What does it feel like to be free?
Free after ten years in prison?

You were lucky
I got life

....

How can I say I'm sorry?

Ten years in prison
Left me alone
My friends were angry
They moved on
My family deserted me
I am no longer married
I have a son I will never see

I read about you in the papers
I read about me in the papers

I thought I saw you today
Every wheelchair cries out your name

Every siren mars a dream
Every dream relives a nightmare
I have thought of you every day for the last ten years
I am 31 and life has been too long
I have no job
No desire
I am sorry for you
And sorry for me
I will never be free

I thought I saw you today
Happy to have a new set of keys
A new chance to drive

Hold Your Breath 100

Squeezed into a room of rules, her head was in a vice
Questions swarmed her muddled mind, answers would be nice
Free verse, Blank verse, Haiku, Riddle, Sonnet, Ballad or something in the middle?
THY NAME SHALL NOT APPEAR ON THE MANUSCRIPT
Alice is not my name.   Alice is not my name.
Alice is not my name is not Alice.
12pt font – What font? – 12pt font – What font? – 12pt font – What font? – 12pt – 12point what?
Only one, only one, only one entry per person.
Only one entry per person only one entry per giant
Only one entry per client only one entry per resident
Only one entry per resident only one entry per client
Only one entry per giant only one entry per person
BSB No. 127630 Bank Account No. 673980 Pin No. ....
Don't give out your number
Don't give out your pin
Don't give out your pin No.
Unless dementia settles in!
DEMENTIA=the eating of too much icecream
One thousand dollars equals one thousand musk sticks
Mirror mirror, class of fools
Is it ok to bend the rules?

Bend the rules − bend the rules
bend the rules − Bend the rules
Rime and mitre − face goes whiter − chest gets tighter
Brain gets lighter
No more than 100 lines   No more than 100 lines
12pt font   ONLY
Open to all − Open to nearly all − Open to residents only −
Not open to non-residents or the computer illiterate − must
be typed − open only to those who have access to a keypad
− typewriter − computer − or friend with such − or access to
access a library − or other such public place that provides
technology for those who do not have or do not have friends
who have it!
Granma can read, Granma can write
Granma can text it, deep in the night
the manuscript! your name must not appear in the manuscript!
If her name was Alice, she'd live in a palace
Instead of these nursing home walls
Her head would be higher, her bed would be drier
And her body not covered in sores
Sign the affidavit sign the affidavit sign the affidavit sign
the affidavit
morethan100 morethan100 morethan100 morethan100
This is not my pin no. Nine three five one

Alice has no account with this bank!
Alice is not real – she has forgotten her pin no.
I dedicate this poem to Maxine – her real name is Alice but I have changed it
I have changed the dates ... I have followed the rules
I had trouble following the rules
This is my own work – I dedicate it to Granma
It cost her 160 cents for a stamp and an envelope
ENTRY IS FREE
Free
Verse
Or rhyme?
Free from what?
What time are you free?
Will it be free for you and me?
What price are you willing to pay for freedom?
As free as a bird in a cage
Freedom in bondage
Like a Fib
Bo na
Cci
Freeisnotfreeisnotfreeisnotfreeisnotfreeisnotfree
It cost her 18 musk sticks to pay for the 9 pages to be photocopied – She kept the receipt

                    I lied about my pin no.
            Some poets avoid paying taxes by staying poor.
        They have no choice.   They think they have no choice.
        They have a choice.   Do they have a choice?
    Cut an' paste it, let's not waste it, she's so old, she can't taste
                                    it
                Seventy Five – your time is running out
    40 is 30   60 is 50
    Must be in by Friday   cut it
    Must be original   paste it
    Only one entry   let's not waste it
                        No one emails
                        No one faxes
                        No one copies it
                        We all pay taxes
What font what font what font what font what font what font
                            what font
                        Is the paper white?
                        Is the paper blue?
                    Is the paper green and gold?
                        What should Alice do?
                        It's hot in here
                        It's hot in here
                    I cannot get fresh air in here
                Turn down the air conditioner dear

It's set at 32
I remember, I remember – YES I DO!
I remember, I remember but I shan't tell you!
S h e f o r g o t t h e s p a c i n g f o r g o t t h e s p a c i n g
32 what? Forgot what it was like at 32? Or was it her address?
She forgot to post it dear
That's why she's in a mess
99...................... Hold your breath.................. 100!

Retirement

The day is drawing to a close
The sun is sinking in the west
The magpies circle far above
And I have some time to rest

I look upon my bushland block
And the tears begin to swell
The place is in an awful state
They say I'll 'ave to sell

Fences down about my knees
And weeds up twice as high
The bracken is so dense in parts
I can 'ardly see the sky

Ducks are dying in the creek
Eels calling out for more
The bloody sow's run off again
I'm sure she smells a boar

Me 'orse is old an' very lame
I 'ave to put him down
But oh the thought of leaving here
And moving into town

I 'aven't seen the dog of late
Mice run freely in the grain
The chooks refuse to 'atch their eggs
There's a bush rat in the drain

But oh the thought of leaving 'ere
And moving to the city
Affects the very heart of me
And fills my soul with pity

I know the roof is leaking
And the plumbin's 'ad its day
The rising damp can't be ignored
But I just want to stay!

I'd miss me birds an' possums
They're me friends why can't they see?
I'd miss the creek and yabbies
And I'd miss me billy tea

But most of all I'd be misplaced
My soul longs for this land
My head is bowed,
I am dismayed
Is this my final stand?

Poppy was a Soldier

Poppy was a soldier
On a boat
In the air force
He didn't see any action
But he was willing to fight for his country
Poppy doesn't get a Gold card cause he didn't see any action
But it wasn't his fault
Poppy worked at the zinc works
Before the regulations
Poppy can't hear a bloody thing
It was so noisy
Before the regulations
No one fought for Poppy
And Poppy never got a Gold card
But he would have fought for his country
It wasn't his fault he didn't see any action
It wasn't his fault they didn't have any regulations
And it wasn't his fault his grandkids never fought for him
But they would have if they'd known

'Hey Mel'

'Hey Mel', I hear you say
'You didn't stop and talk today'
'I know that I was busy but I saw you walk on by'
'Did you have a reason? Was there a reason why?'
How can I say I'm too depressed
To hear your cheer-filled voice
To see your happy countenance, to watch your friends rejoice
I hoped you wouldn't see me as I quickly walked on by
I was very close to tears and I couldn't tell you why
You tell me I'm the happy one – you've never seen me blue
Well today's facade wore thin and I couldn't talk with you
It could just be the hormones causing all the strife
Or the grieving part of death – which is also part of life
Whatever,
It'll pass just like I did today
Tomorrow I'll be normal, and I'll stop and chat away

This Generation

Aunty says we must send a Christmas card
Let her practise forgiveness
I want to hate him
I choose to
Will I be sent to Hell?
What of his four daughters?
They had no choice
Who protected them?
No one!
Not even their poor weak mother
Let him rot in jail
Don't say he's the victim
His father prone to bouts of violence
His father before him an alcoholic
Let that curse go Aunty
This generation must account for itself

Mere Hobbyist

The seeds of regret
Fell beside a river
The river nurtured them
Wild and inviting thoughts splashed up from the rocks
Spilling onto the river bank
Soaking their roots
Feeding them thoughts of freedom
Turning them lush and palatable

The river carried their perfume to me
And I desired their knowledge
I sought through my mind, until the river became clear
Reaching in, I grabbed recklessly at the foliage
But it was beyond my reach
Struggling for liberty, I tried again and again
Until all hope was gone and I cried a river
Humbled, I knelt beside the flowing waters and made a harvest

I bathed naked in the river and
Bore my soul to the life giver
No one saw me
And there was no shame

I took the harvest to the market
Where you called me a hobbyist
Because I was old
But you are naive and your mouth has not yet savoured regret

You labelled me such
Because your craft is your breath
Both pleasure and pressure are your companions
To create is the essence of your survival
And you flourish like the perfected water lily on a warm lake
Spreading your beauty abundantly over popular shores
Spilling your harmonious colours into creeks and rivers
Oh how I fill with pleasure at the sound of your voice

Call me tardy or late
But my beginning was delayed
And the path already strewn with debris and discouragement
My feet bruised and bleeding, with no place to rest
I had to work with my hands
Suppress my imagination
Never allow my dreams to surface
So practised was I that it became second nature
And without thought I denied myself

More than was necessary
Always being available for you
Growing side by side
Together and apart
Now allow my passion to weave its tendrils into your world once more
Let the vines creep along, speaking quietly of my forbidden love
Let the blossoms fall as carpet under our feet
Let never the splendour of age be seen as bitter or discontented

I wish you well
You inspire me
With your beauty and your bluntness

Hobby or not it shall invade me
Until I'm overwhelmed
Until my words become compulsive
Until my alias speaks
And I am no longer an old woman looking for success
But your equal
Where age is irrelevant
And we sit shoulder to shoulder

Albeit mine are more rounded than yours

My People, Birth and Celebrations

What I really want for Christmas

What I really want for Christmas
Is a housemaid for a year
One who washes dishes
And cleans up everywhere

But I'll be happy with a tea towel
Cos I know the money's tight
And I know you'll stand beside me
As I use it every night

What I really want for Christmas
Is a cruise on a big ship
Where I can put my feet up
And watch the dolphins dip

Where exotic lands can pass me by
Or I can go ashore
And watch exotic dancers
While I eat exotic boar

But I'll be happy with a basket
A melon or a peach
And you can watch me carry it
As we walk along the beach

What I really want for Christmas
Is a new and shiny car
One that's really sporty
No rack or towing bar

But I'll be happy with the bus pass
That you buy me every year
And I know it saves us money
Yes I know that cars are dear

What I really want for Christmas
Is a man to prune the roses
To spread a bit of compost
And fix up all the hoses

But I'll be happy with a spade
Cos I know you'll buy the best
And you say, 'It's good to be outdoors
A change is like a rest!'

And now I'm saving money dear
Look what I've bought you
Some tickets to movies
And my mother's coming too

Avocado Kisses

Immi's 1st birthday

Little baby wishes
And avocado kisses
Sharing sweet sultanas
And squishy ripe bananas

Lovely little memories
That stick in Granma's mind
Open up a picture book
To see what we can find

Imogen imagine
All the places we will go
The park with all the swings and things
Where plants and children grow

Where the wind may fluff our hair
And the sand may fill our pockets
Where castles, boats and kings and queens
Take flight in sandy rockets

Imogen imagine
All the songs we'll sing together
Perhaps we'll splash in puddles
And brave all sorts of weather

But for now let's be content
With little baby wishes
Squishy ripe bananas
And avocado kisses

Birth

Life is a continuum
What stops the flow to make this birth so special?
Is this child more worthy than the one born of a homeless
whore in the slums?
She is desired
Planned
She will have more gifts
Life will be easier
Will she know that?
Will she know how much we love her because we love her mother?
Will she struggle with moral issues?
Placed upon her by our system
Unwritten laws
Social conformities
Generational conditionings
Will she be happy?
Will she care about the baby conceived by violence?
And born without choice

Sitting Here Waiting

Sitting here, waiting, biding my time
Waiting for words to fill up this rhyme
My belly's so large, so huge and so round
I'm finding it hard to reach for the ground
Each morning my feet seem further away
My laces untied again for the day
My nails need cutting but they'll have to wait
Till the baby is born, I hope he's not late
He's been moving around day in and day out
Kicking and boxing and climbing about
They're meant to go quiet before they are due
But this one's not quiet – he's as active as two!
They think he could be four kilos – what fun
(I thought it was hard just birthing one)
Well back to the doc's again in a week
For a push and a prod and bit of a peek
The blood pressure's good the sample is fine...
So I'm sitting here waiting – just biding my time!

I've Been Christmas Shopping

I've been Christmas shopping
And I haven't left the house
I just turned on my computer
Went click, click with the mouse!

Bought fairy lights and candy canes
From a factory outlet sale
They guaranteed delivery
If I used the local mail

I put pens and paints and pencils
In a virtual shopping cart
I know the kids will love me
Cos they're really into art

I bought some apples from the Huon
For six dollars ninety-eight
The e-man said for two more bucks
He'd drop them at my gate!

For Nan I bought some chickens
For a family overseas
She'll appreciate the sentiments
(Last year I gave her cheese)

Christmas just got easier
Now everyone's on line
I can purchase almost anything
From bathers down to wine

No bulging bags or wallets
No parking tickets please
No queueing for the bargains
Shopping's such a breeze

The shops can send me anything
It isn't very hard
And all I have to give them
Is the number on this card!

See this?

It's satisfaction streaming from my smug face
I've discovered an easier, cheaper and even more convenient way of doing an otherwise draining activity

Imagine clicking a button and having all your desires dropped at your front door
It's undeniably a positive experience

No parking issues
No bulging wallet
Not even the inevitable parcel juggling routine

My new, convenient alternative has altered my Christmas Shopping forever!

How exciting will it be for the kids when they discover all the
Beaut things I've managed to acquire
And Mum, the woman who has it all... she'll be chuffed to know she's received the gift of compassion – A chicken for the underprivileged
Local or global I love internet shopping!

Actually, I've made so many purchases I don't even need my card to recite the numbers from it

Best Intentions

The things I'd do for Christmas
Were really rather grand
I had the best intentions
But they didn't go as planned

First I'd make some biscuits
For the people in our street
I'd say 'howdy' to our neighbours
A sort of meet and greet

But the oven was too hot
The first batch rather burnt
The second batch I dropped
Beautiful – they weren't

So I started making jam
I had a lot of berries
Currants, red and black
And half a case of cherries

I'd collected lots of jam jars
Made them pretty for the 'Rellies'
Perhaps I'd strain the currants
And turn them into jellies

But alas I had an accident
As I was climbing down the stairs
And the sound of smashing jam jars
Is still ringing in my ears

It was the bikes I tripped on
They threw me for a six
As I stumbled through the handle bars
I knew I's in a fix

Hindsight is a marvellous thing
For where not to store the bikes
'Tis a shame it never happens
Before disaster strikes

The jars continued smashing
Like shrapnel as they went
I could feel my body oozing stuff
I thought my life was spent

As I began to yell for help
I tried to sit up higher
'Twas then I saw the kitchen smoke
I'd set the jam on fire

My neighbour called the fireman
Bless her caring heart
No more jam for me I said
It gave me such a start

I had the best intentions
As I often do
But it can be a harder task
To see a project through

Now I am no quitter
But it's hard to cook in a plaster
And with the stitches and the skin grafts
I feel like a disaster

So I'll leave it for awhile
Till the swelling gives relief
And the house has been refurbished
And they've fixed my broken teeth

I had the best intentions
But it didn't work for me
So I'll try again next year
Just you wait and see!

Not Quite Educated

Memoirs of the undiagnosed Dyslexic

Note book
Thoughts exposed too easily – too confronting
Never write on the first page
Start in the centre – hidden – more comfortable
Especially if the book has staples
Open staples – remove page – destroy unnoticed
The extremely intimate act of writing cannot be flaunted for criticism or judgement
Inadequacies must be kept hidden
Deepest thoughts never revealed
Never seek the root cause of fears and failures or joys and successes
Is there a name ending in 'phobic'?
Discovery would normalize the individual – diminish unfounded self-indulgence
Childish diaries kept for limited intervals
The urge to destroy overwhelming
What if someone reads it?
What if they believe what I thought at that moment was for now and forever?
A conscience too sensitive for its own good
The teacher addressing the unnamed culprit for some misdemeanour
Guilt ridden but innocent
Beautiful note books

Softly coloured pages
Decorated tastefully with floral edges, and splashed lightly
with words of wisdom
Lie blank unused in a bedside drawer
Beckoning to be filled with exciting and happy memories
Spoiled by fears of spelling mistakes and cross outs
Distressed by forms to be filled – unable to study
Poems ironically enabling expression – whipped up in an
instant – hesitation diminished
Recollection of favourite quotes Walt Whitman's "Do I contradict
myself, very well then, I contradict myself. I am large, I contain
multitudes."
I am my own normal
I am acceptable and beautiful
The feeling of success lingers for a moment
But will fade to a dull memory as quickly as an overused
razor blade

My dilemma
Press Send
Or Delete?

I want to be a poet

I want to be a poet
But I don't know how to know it
You know
I don't know how to know it when you are

Naturally I'm mum
It comes from being one
But what makes a man a poet isn't clear

Do I need to write a book?
List the classes that I took
Make you laugh or cry or even feel despair?

I sit here watching birds
Writing down these words
As they flit about the trees in front of me
In life they take a chance
They like to sing and dance
And I feel it's such a lovely place to be

But I'm not an ornithologist
Or an anthropologist
I'm just relaxing with some feathered company

I want to be a poet
But I don't know how to know it
You know
I don't know how to know it when you are

Predicate Etiquette

Euphemisms, idioms, metaphors and similes
Spoonerisms, superlatives, syntax and redundancies

Do I need to know the meaning before I can write an essay?
Or is it just a screening test to keep my mind in disarray?

Positive, progressive, possessive or comparative
Expressive or imperative, reflective or a narrative

I'm so completely full of adjectives
(I think I need some laxatives!)

Infinite and definite, predicate and irony
Homonym and acronym are they a form of tyranny?

If I could grasp the concept of the meaning of these terms
Would I be a better writer or an apple full of worms?

To intimidate or educate by passing an exam?
Will it make me more intelligent or fill my head with spam?

I'd like to be impressive, expressive and compulsive
But the logistics of linguistics to me are just repulsive!

I Often Got My Letters Wrong

I often got my letters wrong
I'd done it all my life
It frustrated all my teachers
And landed me in strife

'Read what's there!' My mum would say
Stop guessing at the word
Discouragement and criticism
Were all I ever heard

I didn't know the variance
Between a t-h and an f
Between a lion and a line
They thought that I was deaf

They sent me to the doctor
Cos I wet the bed at night
I couldn't tell the difference
Between my left hand or my right

Things are different now
Although some things are the same
I sometimes get my letters wrong
But I no longer feel the shame

I have three dyslexic children
And all of them are bright
Sometimes they get the letters wrong
Sometimes they get them right

I love my kids and teach my kids
And one thing I know for sure
I will not mock or laugh at them
When reading is a chore

Precipitation

The cloud is too full
It cannot hold any more information
The words are spilling over – falling from the sky
Everywhere I look I see them
Floating like snow flakes
Drizzling like a wet day

Flashing like lightning bolts in a thunderstorm
They swell upon the footpath and begin to clog the gutters
I see old people tripping over them
Young kids screaming – with delight – picking up words forbidden to use at home
Words and phrases that escape their intellectual abilities
I see literary scholars' and poets' hands raised to the sky
– waiting to catch the perfect expression – the line that will bring them brilliance

In that moment
They grasp all that they desire
Take it home
Write it down
And store it in the cloud

The Bookcase – A Collective Noun in a Thousand Words

Once upon a bookcase by an old and dusty bed
There dozed a stack of nursery tales many years unread

A chamber overlooked by domestic servant's broom
The occupant had locked the door on exiting the room

For years it sat unnoticed by everyone who passed
Till one enchanted evening when it was found at last

It was a curious grandchild that came across the key
And tried a hundred doors or more in search of mystery

When eventually the key began to turn the tired lock
I heard the chime of midnight strike from the hallway clock

The child undiscouraged entered through the ancient door
Opened up the curtains, let moonlight drench the floor

Then she did the strangest thing, quite unlike herself
Pulled down a dozen books or so from off that dusty shelf

With an open hand she let them fall roughly to her feet
Mesmerised by muffled sounds of an accidental beat

The dust swirled about her as she climbed upon the bed
Particles rearranging as the pillow sought her head

Book Folk started forming where the pages tumbled open
The room a hum of noises as voices now were spoken

Young Heidi was the first of the Book Folk to appear
Magically emerging from the swirling dusty air

Peter followed closely from off the typeset page
He'd been tending Grandpa's goats as they grazed on alpine sage

Laura and her sister Mary were on their way to school
Fair Mary quite reluctant to break the golden rule

Laura wasn't worried – it was just a bit of fun
She knew they would retire with the rising of the sun

But if they could get the key from the child's sweaty hand
Book Folk would have a victory for all of nursery land

Their door would be unlocked – they'd change their destiny
They'd never have to wait at all for fate to find the key

Laura stopped and looked around to establish who was here
Tom Sawyer was excited and grinned from ear to ear

He hadn't seen young Mary for quite the longest time He'd often
thought about her – as he led his 'life of crime'

Jack appeared bewildered as he wandered through the pile
Laura hoped he still had beans – she'd not seen him for a while

Then they heard the music and let out a rousing cry
Last they'd heard of Milligan was the graveyard back in Rye

They gathered at the bedpost – the child now asleep
Six young 'uns and a poet's voice – their hearts began to leap

All seemed conceivable to make the counterpane in time
Before the sun ascended or the poet lost his rhyme

Jack took out his magic beans – Heidi planted them in dust
Peter looked for water – precipitation was a must

'There Are Holes in the Sky' by 'Spike' T. A. Milligan
The holes were rather small but the drops could still get in

They dripped into the teapot, from the land of Ning Nang Nong
Magic in the air made the beans grow fast 'n strong

The children formed a circle as the beans began to grow
They twisted round the bed leg weaving to and fro

'Come on,' said Laura taking Mary by the hand
'Let's climb and take that key for all of Nursery Land!'

Mary cried reluctantly, 'We're tardy now for school
Teacher will be angry if we stop to play the fool.'

'That's how it always is,' said Tom broadening up his grin
'Come back with me to my place – I'm sure you'll fit right in'

Mary went from white to red, scarlet in the face
Intertwining books to her was an absolute disgrace

'The irony of that,' said Tom, 'is you are here right now
Planting little Jackie's seeds – which were once a skinny cow'

'That's enough!' said Laura 'let's not waste our words tonight'
(Though anything is possible, if you buy the copyright!)

With youthful ease the children climbed almost to the top
When suddenly the bean stalk moved, our heroes had to stop

Peering up the swaying vine found a giant climbing down
Jack let out a woeful groan and Tom said with a frown

'We nearly had our victory – who let that monster out?!'
A draught had stirred the pages and turned them all about

The children scurried down towards the shelter of their books
No time for glancing back or taking second looks

No time for repetition or vain redundancy
To say it twice would be a waste, otiose tautology

'Where's Jack's axe?' charged Heidi – filled with battle cry
Then she saw her grandpa from the corner of her eye

'Get yourselves a wiggle on, can't hold back this axe for long
Send forth the poet's voice, raise up a chopping song'

The old man poised his axe as the children scurried past
Then with many years of practise he gave that axe a blast

As the poet's voice rang out to the tune of chomping 'Teeth'
The vine began to curl about to form a giant wreath

And all was done ... and all was gone ... and the Book Folk disappeared
As dawning rays of ordinary transformed the room to red

When at last the girl awoke 'twas seven in the morning
Sir Cockerel of the Courtyard was screeching out his warning

The key was in her hand – the dust had settled down
The bookcase ...
      Was once more ...
           Just a sad ... 'collective noun'

Run On

She received his paper
With fear and trepidation
She'd watched him write 2000 words
With no thought of punctuation

Line after line of 'buts' and 'ands'
A miracle of conjunctions
This of course is very well
If the sentence functions

But on it ran and on it ran
Till her lungs began to fail
And as she gasped for air to breathe
Her complexion turned quite pale

After 'but' and 'and' and 'though'
Came 'until', 'therefore', 'unless'
'Except' 'because' and 'wherefore'
Her mind became a mess

Frustration raged about her
(She thought about it after)
But instead she filled her lungs again
And rocked the room with laughter

The subject she had set for him
The one that he had bent
Was 'Is the period necessary
In the school environment?'

Procrastination

Procrastination – now let me think
It is indeed an art
To find excuse to not to do
To stall or not to start

I find myself surrounded
By all the have to dos
Washing, dishes, vacuuming
Scrubbing muddy shoes

But instead of getting in there
Sleeves and all rolled up
I'm curled up here, with pen an' page
 And of course another 'cup'

The sink is begging for attention
But I'll give my friend a call
Find out if she's found a house
Or if they'll move at all

The phone is great for my delays
I can talk for hours
But it doesn't clean the toilets
Or the bathrooms or the showers

There are photos out of albums
Kids' clothing to sort out
The fridge has frosted over
The laundry hangs about

The garbage sends an odour
That beckons me for sure
Although, I think I'm getting used to it
So for now I'll just ignore

If I move and wake the babe
My peace will surely shatter
The mess will still be here tomorrow
So does it really matter?

Perhaps I'll do it later
I'll just check my emails now
There may be inspiration there
A link to show me how

Then I'll rearrange the pantry
And try to catch that mouse
Who's been nibbling all the packets
In my not so tidy house?

Just a Mum

'I'm just a mum,' she said
As she picked him off the floor
Pulled him back a bit
And shut the outside door

'I'm just a mum,' she said
Like it wasn't such a deal
She tickled bub beneath the chin
And listened to him squeal

'I'm just a mum,' she said
As she counted out the plates
Cut up all the carrot sticks
And pitted Chinese dates

'I'm just a mum,' she said
As she pulled out errant weeds
Tidied up the vegie patch
And planted lettuce seeds

'I'm just a mum,' she said
As she hung out soggy clothes
Picked up wayward pegs
And wiped the baby's nose

'What!' I said, with face quite red
'You're the pillar of our nation
What do mean you don't get paid
For sick leave or vacation?'

'I can't believe there's no stress leave
Or superannuation!
How come it is you've been ignored
For such a great vocation?'

'I'm just a mum,' she said
As she began the baby sway
'No one's ever thought of it
In any other way'

The Author

Demelza is an emerging writer who loves words, weekends and waffles. She lives with her extended family in a converted petrol station above a convict built tunnel where she trades coffee for kale, prefers paper to plastic and squeezes writing around copious commitments. Her first incredible novel All the Birds of the Air was successfully published in 2017, and is available on Amazon. Demelza is a Tasmanian citizen who escaped from New Zealand late last century. She now considers herself as Australian as Pavlova.

Colophon

Not Quite Tasmanian was originally published as *Not Quite*, one of 113 books commissioned by A Published Event (Justy Phillips and Margaret Woodward) for The People's Library 2018. Presented in partnership with Salamanca Arts Centre, Hobart, Tasmania.

Not Quite Tasmanian copyright © Demelza 2021.

All rights reserved. No part of this publication may be reproduced, copied or transmitted for commercial gain in any form whatsoever without the prior consent of the author.
Although the author has made every effort to ensure that the information in this book was correct at press time, the author and publisher do not assume and hereby disclaim any liability to any party for any loss, damage, or disruption caused by errors or omissions, whether such errors or omissions result from negligence, accident, or any other cause.

Copy Editing: Kol Sason Press, Ruth Amos.

www.ingramcontent.com/pod-product-compliance
Lightning Source LLC
Chambersburg PA
CBHW020324010526
44107CB00054B/1966